PJ AND FRIENDS
SAY NIGHTY NIGHT

WRITTEN AND ILLUSTRATED BY
LAURA TYLER SAINZ

CITIOFBOOKS, INC.
3736 Eubank NE Suite A1
Albuquerque, NM 87111-3579
www.citiofbooks.com
Hotline: 1 (877) 389-2759
Fax: 1 (505) 930-7244

Ordering Information:
Quantity sales. Special discounts are available on quantity purchases by corporations, associations, and others. For details, contact the publisher at the address above.

Printed in the United States of America.
ISBN-13: Paperback   979-8-89391-153-4
          eBook   979-8-89391-154-1

Library of Congress Control Number: 2024911560

**PJ and Friends Say Nighty Night
Written and Illustrated by
Laura Tyler Sainz**

Help PJ say goodnight to his ranch friends.

Dedicated to my grandchildren and all the children that have been part of my life.

Honk Hi!
I'm "PJ" short for Petey Junior.
I wonder if you would help me say
Nighty Night to my ranch friends?
Let's go!

As the sun sets on the ranch, the chickens begin to make
their way to the chicken coop to say,
"Nighty Night"

cock-
a-doodle
do !
Bock! Bock!

The roosters, "El Capitan" and "Al-B" roost by the door to the coop while Lacy, Sparkles and the other hens climb onto their roost and tuck their beaks under their wings.
"Nighty Night Chickens!"
Nighty Night, bock bock "PJ!" They say back.

Cows sleep mostly lying down.
"Nighty Night Rumpy!"

I like to chew my cud to fall asleep says, Rumpy!
"Nighty Night PJ, Moo!"

Stella the Paint pony can sleep lying down or standing up but, she mostly sleeps lying down.
"Nighty Night Stella!"

"I like to have a little bit of hay before I go to sleep”
says, Stella. “Nom Nom Nighty Night PJ!”

The sheep sleep lying down mostly,
but only for short naps.
Sometimes, when Coyotes howl nearby, Ramsey the
Mouflon ram and his friends take turns sleeping.

The sheep dogs Famous, Shiner and Star keep watch at night and bark at coyotes and other predators to keep them away while my ranch friends and I sleep.
"Nighty Night sheep dogs!"

"Nighty, Night PJ, say the sheep dogs!"

Owe! Yip! Yip! Yip!

Daddy Petey, Mama Pearl and I are peacocks.
We like to sleep way up on top of the hay in the barn or on top of the barn.
Mama Pearl tucks me under her wings as Daddy Petey tells stories of singing peacock songs and dancing peacock dances.

Then Daddy Petey flies up to his roost on the tippy top of the barn and waits until sunrise so he can fly down as the sunlight catches all the beautiful colors of his tail.

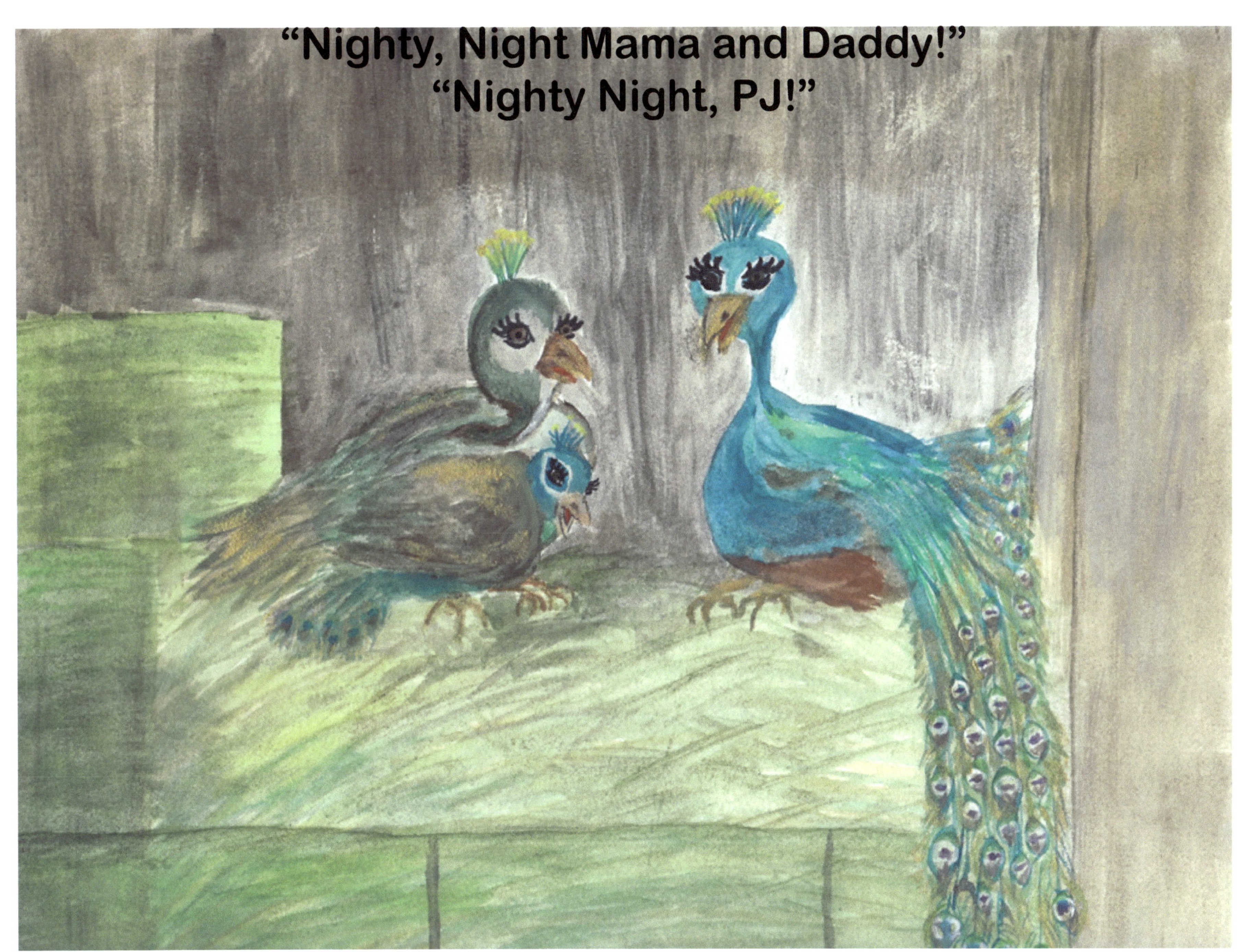

"Nighty, Night Mama and Daddy!"
"Nighty Night, PJ!"